Two (

Selected ٔ ٍ ٍ

Wendy Cope was born in Erith, Kent. After university she worked for fifteen years as a primary school teacher in London. Her first collection of poems, *Making Cocoa for Kinglsey Amis*, was published in 1986. In 1987 she received a Cholmondeley Award for Poetry and in 1995 the American Academy of Arts and Letters Michael Braude Award for light verse.

Praise for Wendy Cope and *Two Cures for Love*:

'An opportunity to read the best of her work in one volume. It reads as freshly as it did when she first found form twenty years ago as the most accomplished and discerning of parodists. Her justly celebrated (and extremely genial) jokes at the expense of T. S. Eliot, John Berryman and Geoffrey Hill among others are testimony to her command of form – seen also in sonnets, triplets, villanelles and ballades. But Cope also has a special second gift, for investing the most ordinary (but important) of emotions – sentimental memories of parents, unrequited love for impossible men – with comic dignity.'
Alan Brownjohn, *Sunday Times*

'Wendy Cope is that very rare thing in the poetry world: a good poet that people actually read.'
Daisy Goodwin, *Daily Telegraph*

'Cope has an extraordinarily canny sense – quite rare among poets – of what will engage the reader's attention.'
Dana Gioia, *Poetry Review*

'It is worth pointing out that without the heart the jokes would not be so good.' Robert Nye, *The Times*

'She should be given a medal for the number of reluctant readers of poetry, of all ages, she's laughingly and tunefully returned to the fold.' *Ambit*

'A jet-age Tennyson.' *London Review of Books*

Saskia Joss

WENDY COPE

Two Cures
for Love

Selected Poems 1979–2006

faber and faber

First published in 2008
by Faber and Faber Limited
Bloomsbury House, 74–77 Great Russell Street, London WC1B 3DA
This paperback edition published in 2010

Typeset by Faber and Faber Limited
Printed in Great Britain by Martins the Printers

A CIP record for this book
is available from the British Library

ISBN 978-0-571-24078-4

4 6 8 10 9 7 5 3

Contents

Preface

My first collection of poems, *Making Cocoa for Kingsley Amis*, has featured on a couple of A-level syllabuses in recent years. When I first learned about this I was pleased to have been chosen by the examination boards but I did have some doubts about the suitability of the book for school pupils. It includes a number of parodies and other literary jokes that can't mean much to readers who haven't encountered the works they refer to. Sixth-form students might have read Wordsworth and T. S. Eliot but I didn't think many of them would be qualified to appreciate a parody of Craig Raine or Geoffrey Hill.

Some of my visits to schools confirmed these misgivings. In one school the pupils had been encouraged to look in my poem 'Budgie Finds His Voice' for evidence of my attitude to environmental issues. They hadn't understood that the poem is a parody of Ted Hughes. When I explained this they were disappointed and tried to argue that it might, none the less, say something about Wendy Cope's views on pollution and global warming. I had to be very firm. And I was uncomfortable, because the last thing I want to do is undermine teachers in front of their students.

The idea for this book grew out of that experience and others like it. It seemed to me that some notes would be helpful to teachers and students, and might be appreciated by other readers too. Some teachers and other readers suggested that a wider selection of my work in one volume would be useful, so I have chosen poems from all three of my collections, together with a few new ones. I've also included a small number of poems that, for one reason or another, were omitted from earlier books but now seem to me worth publishing here.

The usual practice, when putting together a selection of one's poems, is to group together poems that originally appeared in the same collection. I didn't want to do that. My collections are miscellanies. Keeping poems together just because they originally appeared together would have made no sense and I am glad of the opportunity to re-arrange them here. Anyone who wants to know which book a poem first appeared in can find that information in the notes.

When my second and third books were published some reviewers, understandably assuming that all the poems were new, came to erroneous conclusions about my development. In fact, both those books included poems that could have been in an earlier volume. The notes to this book say when each poem was written. Now and again, going through an old notebook, I find a poem I never got around to typing out but which seems to me worth publishing. Then there are poems that got typed but subsequently forgotten because I decided they were no good. Occasionally, looking at such poems years later, I realise I was wrong. For example, 'Names', published in *Serious Concerns* (1992), was written in the early 1980s and spent a decade in a file labelled 'Failures' because the first person I showed it to didn't like it. That person was not my editor at Faber – the poem didn't get as far as being considered for inclusion in my first book. But at least I didn't throw it away.

Since I easily lose confidence in my work, I have been fortunate in having editors who were willing to spend time helping me decide what to publish. Craig Raine worked with me on the first book, Christopher Reid on the second, and Paul Keegan on the third (and on this selection). I thank them for their patience and their advice. And I'd like to take this opportunity to thank Blake Morrison, whose evening classes at Goldsmiths College I attended in the late 1970s and early 1980s. Blake's excellent teaching and his encouragement were of great importance in helping me to become a publishable poet. Thanks, too, to Lachlan Mackinnon, for re-reading many of my poems and helping me put this book together.

Wendy Cope

Two Cures for Love

By the Round Pond

You watch yourself. You watch the watcher too –
A ghostly figure on the garden wall.
And one of you is her, and one is you,
If either one of you exists at all.

How strange to be the one behind a face,
To have a name and know that it is yours,
To be in this particular green place,
To see a snail advance, to see it pause.

You sit quite still and wonder when you'll go.
It could be now. Or now. Or now. You stay.
Who's making up the plot? You'll never know.
Minute after minute swims away.

The Uncertainty of the Poet

'The Tate Gallery yesterday announced that it had paid £1 million for a Giorgio de Chirico masterpiece, *The Uncertainty of the Poet*. It depicts a torso and a bunch of bananas.' – *Guardian*, 2 April 1985

I am a poet.
I am very fond of bananas.

I am bananas.
I am very fond of a poet.

I am a poet of bananas.
I am very fond,

A fond poet of 'I am, I am' –
Very bananas,

Fond of 'Am I bananas,
Am I?' – a very poet.

Bananas of a poet!
Am I fond? Am I very?

Poet bananas! I am.
I am fond of a 'very'.

I am of very fond bananas.
Am I a poet?

The Sitter

Vanessa Bell, *Nude*, *c.*1922–3, Tate Britain

Depressed and disagreeable and fat –
That's how she saw me. It was all she saw.
Around her, yes, I may have looked like that.
She hardly spoke. She thought I was a bore.
Beneath her gaze I couldn't help but slouch.
She made me feel ashamed. My face went red.
I'd rather have been posing on a couch
For some old rake who wanted me in bed.
Some people made me smile, they made me shine,
They made me beautiful. But they're all gone,
Those friends, the way they saw this face of mine,
And her contempt for me is what lives on.
Admired, well-bred, artistic Mrs Bell,
I hope you're looking hideous in Hell.

Les Vacances

Walter Richard Sickert, *Bathers*, *Dieppe*, 1902,
Walker Art Gallery, Liverpool

Maman et Papa au bord de la mer.
Aujourd'hui il fait beau. I remember it well.
Voilà Armand, in the corner down there,
With Maman et Papa au bord de la mer!
Oh, bored, c'est le mot. I tear out the hair
As we limp through ce livre avec Mademoiselle.
Maman et Papa au bord de la mer.
Il fait beau. I remember it only too well.

Tich Miller

Tich Miller wore glasses
with elastoplast-pink frames
and had one foot three sizes larger than the other.

When they picked teams for outdoor games
she and I were always the last two
left standing by the wire-mesh fence.

We avoided one another's eyes,
stooping, perhaps, to re-tie a shoelace,
or affecting interest in the flight

of some fortunate bird, and pretended
not to hear the urgent conference:
'Have Tubby!' 'No, no, have Tich!'

Usually they chose me, the lesser dud,
and she lolloped, unselected,
to the back of the other team.

At eleven we went to different schools.
In time I learned to get my own back,
sneering at hockey-players who couldn't spell.

Tich died when she was twelve.

Names

She was Eliza for a few weeks
When she was a baby –
Eliza Lily. Soon it changed to Lil.

Later she was Miss Steward in the baker's shop
And then 'my love', 'my darling', Mother.

Widowed at thirty, she went back to work
As Mrs Hand. Her daughter grew up,
Married and gave birth.

Now she was Nanna. 'Everybody
Calls me Nanna,' she would say to visitors.
And so they did – friends, tradesmen, the doctor.

In the geriatric ward
They used the patients' Christian names.
'Lil,' we said, 'or Nanna,'
But it wasn't in her file
And for those last bewildered weeks
She was Eliza once again.

Present

On the flyleaf
of my confirmation present:
'To Wendy with love
from Nanna. Psalm 98.'

I looked it up, eventually –
Cantate Domino.
I knew the first two verses
and skimmed the rest.

Thirty-five years afterwards,
at evensong on Day 19
the choir sings Nanna's psalm.
At last, I pay attention

to the words she chose.
*O sing unto the Lord
a new song*. Nanna,
it is just what I wanted.

On Finding an Old Photograph

Yalding, 1912. My father
in an apple orchard, sunlight
patching his stylish bags;

three women dressed in soft,
white blouses, skirts that brush the grass;
a child with curly hair.

If they were strangers
it would calm me – half-drugged
by the atmosphere – but it does more –

eases a burden
made of all his sadness
and the things I didn't give him.

There he is, happy, and I am unborn.

A Christmas Poem

At Christmas little children sing and merry bells jingle,
The cold winter air makes our hands and faces tingle
And happy families go to church and cheerily they
   mingle
And the whole business is unbelievably dreadful, if
   you're single.

Loss

The day he moved out was terrible –
That evening she went through hell.
His absence wasn't a problem
But the corkscrew had gone as well.

From June to December

1 *Prelude*

It wouldn't be a good idea
To let him stay.
When they knew each other better –
Not today.
But she put on her new black knickers
Anyway.

3 *Summer Villanelle*

You know exactly what to do –
Your kiss, your fingers on my thigh –
I think of little else but you.

It's bliss to have a lover who,
Touching one shoulder, makes me sigh –
You know exactly what to do.

You make me happy through and through,
The way the sun lights up the sky –
I think of little else but you.

I hardly sleep – an hour or two;
I can't eat much and this is why –
You know exactly what to do.

The movie in my mind is blue –
As June runs into warm July
I think of little else but you.

But is it love? And is it true?
Who cares? This much I can't deny:
You know exactly what to do;
I think of little else but you.

5 Some People

Some people like sex more than others –
You seem to like it a lot.
There's nothing wrong with being innocent
   or high-minded
But I'm glad you're not.

6 Going Too Far

Cuddling the new telephone directory
After I found your name in it
Was going too far.

It's a safe bet you're not hugging a phone book,
Wherever you are.

My Lover

For I will consider my lover, who shall remain nameless.

For at the age of 49 he can make the noise of five different kinds of lorry changing gear on a hill.

For he sometimes does this on the stairs at his place of work.

For he is embarrassed when people overhear him.

For he can also imitate at least three different kinds of train.

For these include the London tube train, the steam engine, and the Southern Rail electric.

For he supports Tottenham Hotspur with joyful and unswerving devotion.

For he abhors Arsenal, whose supporters are uncivilised and rough.

For he explains that Spurs are magic, whereas Arsenal are boring and defensive.

For I knew nothing of this six months ago, nor did I want to.

For now it all enchants me.

For this he performs in ten degrees.

For first he presents himself as a nice, serious, liberated person.

For secondly he sits through many lunches, discussing life and love and never mentioning football.

For thirdly he is careful not to reveal how much he dislikes losing an argument.

For fourthly he talks about the women in his past, acknowledging that some of it must have been his fault.

For fifthly he is so obviously reasonable that you are inclined to doubt this.

For sixthly he invites himself round for a drink one evening.

For seventhly you consume two bottles of wine between you.

For eighthly he stays the night.

For ninthly you cannot wait to see him again.

For tenthly this does not happen for several days.

For having achieved his object he turns again to his other interests.

For he will not miss his evening class or his choir practice for a woman.

For he is out nearly all the time.

For you cannot even get him on the telephone.

For he is the kind of man who has been driving women round the bend for generations.

For, sad to say, this thought does not bring you to your senses.

For he is charming.

For he is good with animals and children.

For his voice is both reassuring and sexy.

For he drives an A-registration Vauxhall Astra estate.

For he goes at 80 miles per hour on the motorways.

For when I plead with him he says, 'I'm not going any slower than *this*.'

For he is convinced he knows his way around better than anyone else on earth.

For he does not encourage suggestions from his passengers.

For if he ever got lost there would be hell to pay.

For he sometimes makes me sleep on the wrong side of my own bed.

For he cannot be bossed around.

For he has this grace, that he is happy to eat fish fingers or Chinese takeaway or to cook the supper himself.

For he knows about my cooking and is realistic.

For he makes me smooth cocoa with bubbles on the top.

For he drinks and smokes at least as much as I do.

For he is obsessed with sex.

For he would never say it is overrated.

For he grew up before the permissive society and remembers his adolescence.

For he does not insist it is healthy and natural, nor does he ask me what I would like him to do.

For he has a few ideas of his own.

For he has never been able to sleep much and talks with me late into the night.

For we wear each other out with our wakefulness.

For he makes me feel like a light-bulb that cannot switch itself off.

For he inspires poem after poem.

For he is clean and tidy but not too concerned with his appearance.

For he lets the barber cut his hair too short and goes round looking like a convict for a fortnight.

For when I ask if this necklace is all right he replies, 'Yes, if no means looking at three others.'

For he was shocked when younger team-mates began using talcum powder in the changing room.

For his old-fashioned masculinity is the cause of continual merriment on my part.

For this puzzles him.

Rondeau Redoublé

There are so many kinds of awful men –
One can't avoid them all. She often said
She'd never make the same mistake again:
She always made a new mistake instead.

The chinless type who made her feel ill-bred;
The practised charmer, less than charming when
He talked about the wife and kids and fled –
There are so many kinds of awful men.

The half-crazed hippy, deeply into Zen,
Whose cryptic homilies she came to dread;
The fervent youth who worshipped Tony Benn –
'One can't avoid them all,' she often said.

The ageing banker, rich and overfed,
Who held forth on the dollar and the yen –
Though there were many more mistakes ahead,
She'd never make the same mistake again.

The budding poet, scribbling in his den
Odes not to her but to his pussy, Fred;
The drunk who fell asleep at nine or ten –
She always made a new mistake instead.

And so the gambler was at least unwed
And didn't preach or sneer or wield a pen
Or hoard his wealth or take the Scotch to bed.
She'd lived and learned and lived and learned but then
There are so many kinds.

Bloody Men

Bloody men are like bloody buses –
You wait for about a year
And as soon as one approaches your stop
Two or three others appear.

You look at them flashing their indicators,
Offering you a ride.
You're trying to read the destinations,
You haven't much time to decide.

If you make a mistake, there is no turning back.
Jump off, and you'll stand there and gaze
While the cars and the taxis and lorries go by
And the minutes, the hours, the days.

Valentine

My heart has made its mind up
And I'm afraid it's you.
Whatever you've got lined up,
My heart has made its mind up
And if you can't be signed up
This year, next year will do.
My heart has made its mind up
And I'm afraid it's you.

Nine-line Triolet

Here's a fine mess we got ourselves into,
My angel, my darling, true love of my heart
Etcetera. Must stop it but I can't begin to.
Here's a fine mess we got ourselves into –
Both in a spin with nowhere to spin to,
Bound by the old rules in life and in art.
Here's a fine mess we got ourselves into,
(I'll curse every rule in the book as we part)
My angel, my darling, true love of my heart.

Favourite

When they ask me, 'Who's your favourite poet?'
I'd better not mention you,
Though you certainly are my favourite poet
And I like your poems too.

Another Unfortunate Choice

I think I am in love with A. E. Housman,
Which puts me in a worse-than-usual fix.
No woman ever stood a chance with Housman
And he's been dead since 1936.

As Sweet

It's all because we're so alike –
Twin souls, we two.
We smile at the expression, yes,
And know it's true.

I told the shrink. He gave our love
A different name.
But he can call it what he likes –
It's still the same.

I long to see you, hear your voice,
My narcissistic object-choice.

In the Rhine Valley

Die Farben der Bäume sind schön
And the sky's and the river's blue-greys
And the *Burg*, almost lost in the haze.

You're patient. You help me to learn
And you smile as I practise the phrase,
'*Die Farben der Bäume sind schön.*'

October. The year's on the turn –
It will take us our separate ways
But the sun shines. And we have two days.
Die Farben der Bäume sind schön.

Postcards

(commissioned for broadcast by BBC World Service)

At first I sent you a postcard
From every city I went to.
Grüsse aus Bath, aus Birmingham,
Aus Rotterdam, aus Tel Aviv.
Mit Liebe. Cards from you arrived
In English, with many commas.
Hope, you're fine and still alive,
Says one from Hong Kong. By that time
We weren't writing quite as often.

Now we're nearly nine years away
From the lake and the blue mountains,
And the room with the balcony,
But the heat and light of those days
Can reach this far from time to time.
Your latest was from Senegal,
Mine from Helsinki. I don't know
If we'll meet again. Be happy.
If you hear this, send a postcard.

Seeing You

Seeing you will make me sad.
I want to do it anyway.
We can't relive the times we had –
Seeing you will make me sad.
Perhaps it's wrong. Perhaps it's mad.
But we will both be dead one day.
Seeing you will make me sad.
I have to do it anyway.

The Orange

At lunchtime I bought a huge orange –
The size of it made us all laugh.
I peeled it and shared it with Robert and Dave –
They got quarters and I had a half.

And that orange, it made me so happy,
As ordinary things often do
Just lately. The shopping. A walk in the park.
This is peace and contentment. It's new.

The rest of the day was quite easy.
I did all the jobs on my list
And enjoyed them and had some time over.
I love you. I'm glad I exist.

After the Lunch

On Waterloo Bridge, where we said our goodbyes,
The weather conditions bring tears to my eyes.
I wipe them away with a black woolly glove
And try not to notice I've fallen in love.

On Waterloo Bridge I am trying to think:
This is nothing. You're high on the charm and the drink.
But the juke-box inside me is playing a song
That says something different. And when was it wrong?

On Waterloo Bridge with the wind in my hair
I am tempted to skip. *You're a fool.* I don't care.
The head does its best but the heart is the boss –
I admit it before I am halfway across.

The Aerial

The aerial on this radio broke
A long, long time ago,
When you were just a name to me –
Someone I didn't know.

The man before the man before
Had not yet set his cap
The day a clumsy gesture caused
That slender rod to snap.

Love came along. Love came along.
Then you. And now it's ended.
Tomorrow I shall tidy up
And get the radio mended.

Defining the Problem

I can't forgive you. Even if I could,
You wouldn't pardon me for seeing through you.
And yet I cannot cure myself of love
For what I thought you were before I knew you.

Two Cures for Love

1. Don't see him. Don't phone or write a letter.
2. The easy way: get to know him better.

Faint Praise

Size isn't everything. It's what you do
That matters, darling, and you do quite well
In some respects. Credit where credit's due –
You work, you're literate, you rarely smell.
Small men can be aggressive, people say,
But you are often genial and kind,
As long as you can have things all your way
And I comply, and do not speak my mind.
You look all right. I've never been disgusted
By paunchiness. Who wants some skinny youth?
My friends have warned me that you can't be trusted
But I protest I've heard you tell the truth.
Nobody's perfect. Now and then, my pet,
You're almost human. You could make it yet.

Some More Light Verse

You have to try. You see a shrink.
You learn a lot. You read. You think.
You struggle to improve your looks.
You meet some men. You write some books.
You eat good food. You give up junk.
You do not smoke. You don't get drunk.
You take up yoga, walk and swim.
And nothing works. The outlook's grim.
You don't know what to do. You cry.
You're running out of things to try.

You blow your nose. You see the shrink.
You walk. You give up food and drink.
You fall in love. You make a plan.
You struggle to improve your man.
And nothing works. The outlook's grim.
You go to yoga, cry, and swim.
You eat and drink. You give up looks.
You struggle to improve your books.
You cannot see the point. You sigh.
You do not smoke. You have to try.

Differences of Opinion

1 *He Tells Her*

He tells her that the earth is flat –
He knows the facts, and that is that.
In altercations fierce and long
She tries her best to prove him wrong.
But he has learned to argue well.
He calls her arguments unsound
And often asks her not to yell.
She cannot win. He stands his ground.

The planet goes on being round.

2 *Your Mother Knows*

Your mother *knows* the earth's a plane
And, challenged, sheds a martyr's tear.
God give her strength to bear this pain –
A child who says the world's a sphere!

Challenged, she sheds a martyr's tear.
It's bad to make your mother cry
By telling her the world's a sphere.
It's very bad to tell a lie.

It's bad to make your mother cry.
It's bad to think your mother odd.
It's very bad to tell a lie.
All this has been ordained by God.

It's bad to think your mother odd.
The world is round. That's also true.
All this has been ordained by God.
It's hard to see what you can do.

The world is round. That *must* be true.
She's praying, hoping you will change.
It's hard to see what you can do.
Already people find you strange.

She's praying, hoping you will change.
You're difficult. You don't fit in.
Already people find you strange.
You know your anger is a sin.

You're difficult. You don't fit in.
God give her strength to bear this pain.
You know your anger is a sin.
Your mother knows the earth's a plane.

Flowers

Some men never think of it.
You did. You'd come along
And say you'd nearly brought me flowers
But something had gone wrong.

The shop was closed. Or you had doubts –
The sort that minds like ours
Dream up incessantly. You thought
I might not want your flowers.

It made me smile and hug you then.
Now I can only smile.
But, look, the flowers you nearly brought
Have lasted all this while.

On a Train

The book I've been reading
rests on my knee. You sleep.

It's beautiful out there –
fields, little lakes and winter trees
in February sunlight,
every car park a shining mosaic.

Long, radiant minutes,
your hand in my hand,
still warm, still warm.

Being Boring

'May you live in interesting times.' – Chinese curse

If you ask me 'What's new?', I have nothing to say
Except that the garden is growing.
I had a slight cold but it's better today.
I'm content with the way things are going.
Yes, he is the same as he usually is,
Still eating and sleeping and snoring.
I get on with my work. He gets on with his.
I know this is all very boring.

There was drama enough in my turbulent past:
Tears and passion – I've used up a tankful.
No news is good news, and long may it last.
If nothing much happens, I'm thankful.
A happier cabbage you never did see,
My vegetable spirits are soaring.
If you're after excitement, steer well clear of me.
I want to go on being boring.

I don't go to parties. Well, what are they for,
If you don't need to find a new lover?
You drink and you listen and drink a bit more
And you take the next day to recover.
Someone to stay home with was all my desire
And, now that I've found a safe mooring,
I've just one ambition in life: I aspire
To go on and on being boring.

Timekeeping

Late home for supper,
He mustn't seem drunk.
'The pob cluck', he begins,
And knows he is sunk.

The Christmas Life

'If you don't have a real tree, you don't bring the Christmas life
into the house.' – Josephine Mackinnon, aged 8

Bring in a tree, a young Norwegian spruce,
Bring hyacinths that rooted in the cold.
Bring winter jasmine as its buds unfold –
Bring the Christmas life into this house.

Bring red and green and gold, bring things that shine,
Bring candlesticks and music, food and wine.
Bring in your memories of Christmas past.
Bring in your tears for all that you have lost.

Bring in the shepherd boy, the ox and ass,
Bring in the stillness of an icy night,
Bring in a birth, of hope and love and light.
Bring the Christmas life into this house.

30th December

At first I'm startled by the sound of bicycles
Above my head. And then I see them, two swans
Flying in to their runway behind the reeds.

The bridge is slippery, the grass so sodden
That water seeps into my shoes. But now
The sun has come out and everything is calm
And beautiful as the end of a hangover.

Christmas was a muddle
Of turkey bones and muted quarrelling.

The visitors have left.
Solitary walkers smile and tell each other
That the day is wonderful.

If only this could be Christmas now –
These shining meadows,
The hum of huge wings in the sky.

Spared

'That Love is all there is,
Is all we know of Love . . .'
    – Emily Dickinson

It wasn't you, it wasn't me,
Up there, two thousand feet above
A New York street. We're safe and free,
A little while, to live and love,

Imagining what might have been –
The phone call from the blazing tower,
A last farewell on the machine,
While someone sleeps another hour,

Or worse, perhaps, to say goodbye
And listen to each other's pain,
Send helpless love across the sky,
Knowing we'll never meet again,

Or jump together, hand in hand,
To certain death. Spared all of this
For now, how well I understand
That love is all, is all there is.

If I Don't Know

for Louise Kerr

If I don't know how to be thankful enough
for the clusters of white blossom

on our mock orange, which has grown tall
and graceful, come into its own

like a new star just out of ballet school,
and if I don't know what to do

about those spires of sky-blue delphinium,
then what about the way they look together?

And what about the roses, or just one of them –
that solid pinky-peachy bloom

that hollows towards its heart? Outrageous.
I could crush it to bits.

A photograph? A dance to summer?
I sit on the swing and cry.

The rose. The gardenful. The evening light.
It's nine o'clock and I can still see everything.

Tulips

Months ago I dreamed of a tulip garden,
Planted, waited, watched for their first appearance,
Saw them bud, saw greenness give way to colours,
Just as I'd planned them.

Every day I wonder how long they'll be here.
Sad and fearing sadness as I admire them,
Knowing I must lose them, I almost wish them
Gone by tomorrow.

Haiku

A perfect white wine
is sharp, sweet and cold as this:
birdsong in winter.

Haiku:
Looking Out of the Back Bedroom Window without My Glasses

What's that amazing
new lemon-yellow flower?
Oh yes, a football.

The Month of May

'O! the month of May, the merry month of May . . .'
– Thomas Dekker (d. 1632)

The month of May, the merry month of May,
So long awaited, and so quickly past.
The winter's over, and it's time to play.

I saw a hundred shades of green today
And everything that Man made was outclassed.
The month of May, the merry month of May.

Now hello pink and white and farewell grey.
My spirits are no longer overcast.
The winter's over and it's time to play.

Sing 'Fa la la la la,' I dare to say,
(Tried being modern but it didn't last)
'The month of May, the merry month of May.'

I don't know how much longer I can stay.
The summers come, the summers go so fast,
And soon there will be no more time to play.

So *carpe diem*, gather buds, make hay.
The world is glorious. Compare, contrast
December with the merry month of May.
Now is the time, now *is* the time to play.

Leaving

for Dick and Afkham

Next summer? The summer after?
With luck we've a few more years
Of sunshine and drinking and laughter
And airports and goodbyes and tears.

A Nursery Rhyme

as it might have been written by William Wordsworth

The skylark and the jay sang loud and long,
The sun was calm and bright, the air was sweet,
When all at once I heard above the throng
Of jocund birds a single plaintive bleat.

And, turning, saw, as one sees in a dream,
It was a Sheep had broke the moorland peace
With his sad cry, a creature who did seem
The blackest thing that ever wore a fleece.

I walked towards him on the stony track
And, pausing for a while between two crags,
I asked him, 'Have you wool upon your back?'
Thus he bespake. 'Enough to fill three bags.'

Most courteously, in measured tones, he told
Who would receive each bag and where they dwelt;
And oft, now years have passed and I am old,
I recollect with joy that inky pelt.

A Nursery Rhyme

as it might have been written by T. S. Eliot

Because time will not run backwards
Because time
Because time will not run
                    Hickory dickory

In the last minute of the first hour
I saw the mouse ascend the ancient timepiece,
Claws whispering like wind in dry hyacinths.

One o'clock,
The street lamp said,
'Remark the mouse that races towards the carpet.'

And the unstilled wheel still turning
                    Hickory dickory
                    Hickory dickory

dock

Waste Land Limericks

In April one seldom feels cheerful;
Dry stones, sun and dust make me fearful;
Clairvoyantes distress me,
Commuters depress me –
Met Stetson and gave him an earful.

She sat on a mighty fine chair,
Sparks flew as she tidied her hair;
She asks many questions,
I make few suggestions –
Bad as Albert and Lil – what a pair!

III

The Thames runs, bones rattle, rats creep;
Tiresias fancies a peep –
A typist is laid,
A record is played –
Wei la la. After this it gets deep.

IV

A Phoenician called Phlebas forgot
About birds and his business – the lot,
Which is no surprise,
Since he'd met his demise
And been left in the ocean to rot.

V

No water. Dry rocks and dry throats,
Then thunder, a shower of quotes
From the Sanskrit and Dante.
Da. Damyata. Shantih.
I hope you'll make sense of the notes.

A Policeman's Lot

'The progress of any writer is marked by those moments when he manages to outwit his own inner police system.' – Ted Hughes

Oh, once I was a policeman young and merry
                                 (young and merry),
Controlling crowds and fighting petty crime (petty crime),
But now I work on matters literary (litererry)
And I am growing old before my time ('fore my time).
No, the imagination of a writer (of a writer)
Is not the sort of beat a chap would choose
                                 (chap would choose)
And they've assigned me a prolific blighter ('lific blighter) –
I'm patrolling the unconscious of Ted Hughes.

It's not the sort of beat a chap would choose
                                 (chap would choose) –
Patrolling the unconscious of Ted Hughes.

All our leave was cancelled in the lambing season
                                 (lambing season),
When bitter winter froze the drinking trough
                                 (drinking trough),
For our commander stated, with good reason
                                 (with good reason),
That that's the kind of thing that starts him off
                                 (starts him off).
But anything with four legs causes trouble
                                 (causes trouble) –
It's worse than organising several zoos (several zoos),

Not to mention mythic creatures in the rubble
                              (in the rubble),
Patrolling the unconscious of Ted Hughes.

It's worse than organising several zoos (several zoos),
Patrolling the unconscious of Ted Hughes.

Although it's disagreeable and stressful
                              (bull and stressful)
Attempting to avert poetic thought ('etic thought),
I could boast of times when I have been successful
                              (been successful)
And conspiring compound epithets were caught
                              ('thets were caught).
But the poetry statistics in this sector (in this sector)
Are enough to make a copper turn to booze
                              (turn to booze)
And I do not think I'll make it to inspector (to inspector)
Patrolling the unconscious of Ted Hughes.

It's enough to make a copper turn to booze
                              (turn to booze) -
Patrolling the unconscious of Ted Hughes.

                              after W. S. Gilbert

Budgie Finds His Voice

from *The Life and Songs of the Budgie* by Jake Strugnell

God decided he was tired
Of his spinning toys.
They wobbled and grew still.

When the sun was lifted away
Like an orange lifted from a fruit-bowl

And darkness, blacker
Than an oil-slick,
Covered everything forever

And the last ear left on earth
Lay on the beach
Deaf as a shell

And the land froze
And the seas froze

'Who's a pretty boy then?' Budgie cried.

Uisce Beatha

Deft, practised, eager,
Your fingers twist the metal cap.
Late into the moth-infested night
We listen to soft scrapings
Of bottle-top on ridged glass,

The plash and glug of amber liquid
Streaming into tumblers, inches deep.
Life-water. Fire-tanged
Hard-stuff. Gallons of it,
Sipped and swigged and swallowed.

Whiskey: its terse vowels belie
The slow fuddling and mellowing,
Our guttural speech slurring
Into warm, thick blather,
The pie-eyed, slug-witted slump

Into soused oblivion –
And the awakening. I long
For pure, cold water as the pump
Creaks in the yard. A bucket
Clatters to the ground. Is agony.

The Lavatory Attendant

Slumped on a chair, his body is an S
That wants to be a minus sign.

His face is overripe Wensleydale
Going blue at the edges.

In overalls of sacerdotal white
He guards a row of fonts

With lids like eye-patches. Snapped shut
They are castanets. All day he hears

Short-lived Niagaras, the clank
And gurgle of canescent cisterns.

When evening comes he sluices a thin tide
Across sand-coloured lino,

Turns Medusa on her head
And wipes the floor with her.

Duffa Rex

I

King of the primeval avenues, the municipal parklands:
architect of the Tulse Hill Poetry Group: life and soul of
the perennial carousals: minstrel: philatelist: long-serving
clerical officer: the friend of everyone who's anyone.

'Pack it in,' said Duffa, 'and buy me a drink.'

II

He digs for the salt-screw, buried in crepitant spud-slivers.
Speaks of his boyhood in the grunder's yarg, the
unworked cork-bundles, coagulations of nurls.

The mockery of his companions is unabated. It is the
king's round, they urge. His hoard is overripe for
commerce.

One by one he draws coins to the light; examines them:
exemplary silver, his rune stones. Treasure accrued in a
sparse week, to be invested in precious liquid.

God and the Jolly Bored Bog-Mouse

Strugnell's entry for the Arvon/Observer Poetry
Competition 1980. The competition was judged by Ted Hughes,
Philip Larkin, Seamus Heaney and Charles Causley.

God tried to teach Mouse how to sing.
'Piss off! I'm not the sort.'
Mouse squelched away across the bog.
'It's jolly cold,' he thought.

Stone-numb, Mouse watched the ice-bright stars,
Decided they were boring.
Cradled in roots and sodden turf,
Soon he was jolly snoring.

Mouse dreamed a Universe of Blood,
He dreamed a shabby room,
He dreamed a dank hole in the earth,
(Back to the jolly womb).

Mouse tried to vomit up his guts
Then got up for a pee.
A comet pulsed across the sky –
He didn't jolly see.

from Strugnell's Sonnets

for D. M. Thomas

I

The expense of spirits is a crying shame,
So is the cost of wine. What bard today
Can live like old Khayyám? It's not the same –
A loaf and Thou and Tesco's Beaujolais.
I had this bird called Sharon, fond of gin –
Could knock back six or seven. At the price
I paid a high wage for each hour of sin
And that was why I only had her twice.
Then there was Tracey, who drank rum and Coke,
So beautiful I didn't mind at first
But love grows colder. Now some other bloke
Is subsidising Tracey and her thirst.
I need a woman, honest and sincere,
Who'll come across on half a pint of beer.

Not only marble, but the plastic toys
From cornflake packets will outlive this rhyme:
I can't immortalise you, love – our joys
Will lie unnoticed in the vault of time.
When Mrs Thatcher has been cast in bronze
And her administration is a page
In some O-level text-book, when the dons
Have analysed the story of our age,
When travel firms sell tours of outer space
And aeroplanes take off without a sound
And Tulse Hill has become a trendy place
And Upper Norwood's on the underground
Your beauty and my name will be forgotten –
My love is true, but all my verse is rotten.

'At the moment, if you're seen reading poetry in a train,
the carriage empties instantly.'
– Andrew Motion in a *Guardian* interview

Indeed 'tis true. I travel here and there
On British Rail a lot. I've often said
That if you haven't got the first-class fare
You really need a book of verse instead.
Then, should you find that all the seats are taken,
Brandish your Edward Thomas, Yeats or Pound.
Your fellow-passengers, severely shaken,
Will almost all be loath to stick around.
Recent research in railway sociology
Shows it's best to read the stuff aloud:
A few choice bits from Motion's new anthology
And you'll be lonelier than any cloud.
This stratagem's a godsend to recluses
And demonstrates that poetry has its uses.

Strugnell's Haiku

I

The cherry blossom
In my neighbour's garden – Oh!
It looks really nice.

II

The leaves have fallen
And the snow has fallen and
Soon my hair also ...

III

November evening:
The moon is up, rooks settle,
The pubs are open.

Reading Berryman's *Dream Songs*
at the Writers' Retreat

Wendy went a-swimming. It was dreadful.
One small boy careless under her did surface
and did butt her on the chin.
Of space to swim was hardly any,
fearful shoutings, bodies from the springboard
splash when jumping in.

Why no school? cried agey Wendy
to herself, not loud. Why little beggars
swimming into me on Friday afternoon?
Why not in cage, learn tables?
Out and dress and buy bananas.
Yogurt? No. Need spoon.

Once more to Hawthornden through Scottish fog.
Back up to poet's lair and sit on bed.
Is you bored, Bones, all by youzeself
wif read and write and bein' deep?
Not for a moment.
Now, a little sleep.

Reading Scheme

Here is Peter. Here is Jane. They like fun.
Jane has a big doll. Peter has a ball.
Look, Jane, look! Look at the dog! See him run!

Here is Mummy. She has baked a bun.
Here is the milkman. He has come to call.
Here is Peter. Here is Jane. They like fun.

Go Peter! Go Jane! Come, milkman, come!
The milkman likes Mummy. She likes them all.
Look, Jane, look! Look at the dog! See him run!

Here are the curtains. They shut out the sun.
Let us peep! On tiptoe Jane! You are small!
Here is Peter. Here is Jane. They like fun.

I hear a car, Jane. The milkman looks glum.
Here is Daddy in his car. Daddy is tall.
Look, Jane, look! Look at the dog! See him run!

Daddy looks very cross. Has he a gun?
Up milkman! Up milkman! Over the wall!
Here is Peter. Here is Jane. They like fun.
Look, Jane, look! Look at the dog! See him run!

Proverbial Ballade

Fine words won't turn the icing pink;
A wild rose has no employees;
Who boils his socks will make them shrink;
Who catches cold is sure to sneeze.
Who has two legs must wash two knees;
Who breaks the egg will find the yolk;
Who locks his door will need his keys –
So say I and so say the folk.

You can't shave with a tiddlywink,
Nor make red wine from garden peas,
Nor show a blindworm how to blink,
Nor teach an old racoon Chinese.
The juiciest orange feels the squeeze;
Who spends his portion will be broke;
Who has no milk can make no cheese –
So say I and so say the folk.

He makes no blot who has no ink,
Nor gathers honey who keeps no bees.
The ship that does not float will sink;
Who'd travel far must cross the seas.
Lone wolves are seldom seen in threes;
A conker ne'er becomes an oak;
Rome wasn't built by chimpanzees –
So say I and so say the folk.

Envoi

Dear friends! If adages like these
Should seem banal, or just a joke,
Remember fish don't grow on trees –
So say I and so say the folk.

Exchange of Letters

'Man who is a serious novel would like to hear from a woman is a poem' – classified advertisement, *New York Review of Books*

Dear Serious Novel,

I am a terse, assured lyric with impeccable rhythmic flow, some apt and original metaphors, and a music that is all my own. Some people say I am beautiful.

My vital statistics are eighteen lines, divided into three-line stanzas, with an average of four words per line.

My first husband was a cheap romance; the second was *Wisden's Cricketers' Almanac*. Most of the men I meet nowadays are autobiographies, but a substantial minority are books about photography or trains.

I have always hoped for a relationship with an upmarket work of fiction. Please write and tell me more about yourself.

> Yours intensely
> Song of the First Snowdrop

Dear Song of the First Snowdrop,

Many thanks for your letter. You sound like just the kind of poem I am hoping to find. I've always preferred short, lyrical women to the kind who go on for page after page.

I am an important 150,000-word comment on the dreams and dilemmas of twentieth-century Man. It took six years to attain my present weight and stature but all the twenty-seven publishers I have so far approached have failed to understand me. I have my share of sex and violence and a very good joke in chapter nine, but to no avail. I am sustained by the belief that I am ahead of my time.

Let's meet as soon as possible. I am longing for you to read me from cover to cover and get to know my every word.

Yours impatiently,
Death of the Zeitgeist

Stress

for Henry Thompson, but not about him

He would refuse to put the refuse out.
The contents of the bin would start to smell.
How could she be content? That idle lout
Would drive the tamest woman to rebel.
And, now that she's a rebel, he frequents
The pub for frequent drink-ups with a mate
Who nods a lot whenever he presents
His present life at home as far from great.
The drinking makes his conduct even worse
And she conducts herself like some poor soul
In torment. She torments her friends with verse,
Her protest poems – dreadful, on the whole.
We daren't protest. Why risk an upset when
She's so upset already? I blame men.

An Attempt at Unrhymed Verse

People tell you all the time,
Poems do not have to rhyme.
It's often better if they don't
And I'm determined this one won't.
                              Oh dear.

Never mind, I'll start again.
Busy, busy with my pen . . . cil.
I can do it, if I try –
Easy, peasy, pudding and gherkins.

Writing verse is so much fun,
Cheering as the summer weather,
Makes you feel alert and bright,
'Specially when you get it more or less the way
    you want it.

Making Cocoa for Kingsley Amis

It was a dream I had last week
And some sort of record seemed vital.
I knew it wouldn't be much of a poem
But I love the title.

Sonnet of '68

The uproar's over, and the calls to fight
For freedom, the Utopian fantasies.
We took a fairground ride to Paradise
And afterwards there's nothing more, goodnight.

The fire burnt out. The veterans, turning grey,
Make legends of the beautiful, wild past.
These will stay with us till we breathe our last:
The red flag and the photograph of Che.

So many speeches. There's a silence now.
Each of us walks along the city street
Alone, concerned about his daily bread.

We overreached ourselves a little bit.
Euphoria didn't suit us anyhow.
Those who did not outgrow it – they are dead.

Translated from the German of Harry Oberländer

An Anniversary Poem

10th anniversary of the ordination of the first women priests
in the Church of England in February 1994

Good Christian men and women, let us raise a joyful
    shout:
The C of E is treating us as equals. Just about.

Sister, fetch the fatted calf, and we'll prepare a feast:
You can't become a bishop but you can become a priest.

The mountains skip like rams, the little hills like sheep.
    And why?
Our problem-solving miracle: a bishop who can fly.

Sing, dance, clap your hands, make merry and be glad:
Some men behave atrociously, but most are not too bad.

Bring out the tambourines, and let the trumpet sound:
These years have not been easy but, praise God, you're
    still around,

Brave, forgiving pioneers. May this be your reward:
To grow in strength and beauty in the service of the Lord.

But should there be a woman Primate while I'm still alive,
Oh, then we'll hear the valleys sing, and see the mountains
    jive.

How to Deal with the Press

She'll urge you to confide. Resist.
Be careful, courteous, and cool.
Never trust a journalist.

'We're off the record,' she'll insist.
If you believe her, you're a fool.
She'll urge you to confide. Resist.

Should you tell her who you've kissed,
You'll see it all in print, and you'll
Never trust a journalist

Again. The words are hers to twist,
And yours the risk of ridicule.
She'll urge you to confide. Resist.

'But X is nice,' the publicist
Will tell you. 'We were friends at school.'
Never trust a journalist,

Hostile, friendly, sober, pissed,
Male or female – that's the rule.
When tempted to confide, resist.
Never trust a journalist.

A Hampshire Disaster

'Shock was the emotion of most'
Hampshire Chronicle, 13 May 1994

When fire engulfed the headquarters
Of the Royal Winchester Golf Club
In the early hours of Wednesday morning,
Shock was the emotion of most.

But fear had been the emotion
Of some who saw the flames, and admiration
For the courage and skill of the firefighters
Was another emotion felt.

At the loss of so much history –
Cups, trophies, and honours boards –
Sadness is now the emotion
Of many Winchester golfers.

Stoical resignation was the emotion
Of the club captain, as he told the *Chronicle*
'The next procedure will be to sort out the insurance.
Life must go on.'

Greek Island Triolets

2 *Sartorial*

Why did I buy this Marks and Spencer's T-shirt
And, having done so, fail to take it back?
An average English-frump-beside-the-sea-shirt –
Why did I buy this Marks and Spencer's T-shirt?
I needed something ace. This is a B-shirt,
Fit only to be worn beneath a mac.
Why did I buy this Marks and Spencer's T-shirt?
Shall I wash it once and take it back?

3 *Arboreal*

We hugged a tree last night
And all of us enjoyed it.
Ecstatic, by moonlight,
We hugged a tree last night.
Trees can't put up a fight –
That oak could not avoid it.
We hugged it good and tight –
I hope the tree enjoyed it.

Limerick

A talented young chimpanzee
Was keen to appear on TV.
He wrote to Brooke Bond
But they didn't respond
So he had to become an MP.

The Stickleback Song

'Someone should see to the dead stickleback.'
School inspector to London headteacher

A team of inspectors came round here today,
They looked at our school and pronounced it OK.
We've no need to worry, we shan't get the sack,
But someone should see to the dead stickleback,
Dead stickleback, dead stickleback,
But someone should see to the dead stickleback.

Well, we've got some gerbils, all thumping their tails,
And we've got a tankful of live water-snails,
But there's one little creature we certainly lack –
We haven't a quick or a dead stickleback,
Dead stickleback, dead stickleback,
We haven't a quick or a dead stickleback.

Oh was it a spectre the inspector saw,
The ghost of some poor classroom pet who's no more?
And will it be friendly or will it attack?
We're living in fear of the dead stickleback,
Dead stickleback, dead stickleback,
We're living in fear of the dead stickleback.

Or perhaps there's a moral to this little song:
Inspectors work hard and their hours are too long.
When they overdo it, their minds start to crack
And they begin seeing the dead stickleback,
Dead stickleback, dead stickleback,
And they begin seeing the dead stickleback.

Now all you young teachers, so eager and good,
You won't lose your wits for a few years, touch wood.
But take off as fast as a hare on the track
The day you encounter the dead stickleback.
Dead stickleback, dead stickleback,
The day you encounter the dead stickleback.

Traditional Prize County Pigs

1 *Wessex Saddleback*

A porcine aborigine,
He has no trace of foreign blood.
His ancestors were wild and free
British pigs in British mud.

He's a hardy, outdoor type,
Who's never heard of central heating.
He doesn't whine, he doesn't gripe
But, strong and silent, goes on eating.

2 *Oxfordshire Sandy and Black*

This piggy has a pedigree
That goes way back on Midlands farms.
If she could read her family tree,
She might design a coat of arms.

But she knows nothing of her line,
And lives like any other sow,
Taking care of little swine,
Imprisoned in the here and now.

3 Cornish Lop-eared

A fine white pig of goodly size,
He roots and gobbles from the ground
But when he tries to look around,
His lop ears droop across his eyes.

He doesn't know the world is big
And beautiful. He doesn't try
To wander. He's an easy pig,
Content to stay within his sty.

4 Staffordshire Tamworth Red

If you want to go away
On a summer holiday
And take your pig, make no mistake,
A Tamworth Red's the pig to take.

A pig whose skin is very fair
Will use up all your Ambre Solaire,
And need a hat, and cause concern,
But Tamworths very seldom burn.

5 Orkney Boar

If you should meet an Orkney Boar
A-roaming on an Orkney moor,
Beware. This savage little porker
May attack the English walker.

6 *Lincolnshire Curly Coat*

A pig of pigs. If free to scoff,
He'll seldom leave the feeding-trough,
Expanding till he's almost static
And procreation's problematic.

And that, I guess, is why the breed
By now is very rare indeed.

7 *Gloucestershire Old Spot*

Walking Rorschach tests, Old Spots
Have pure white skin with inky blots
But do not show an interest
In asking what the shapes suggest.

8 *Berkshire Prize Beauty*

Once the standard of perfection
By which other pigs were judged –
Lovely figure, great complexion
Even when her face was smudged.
Just imagine the dejection
As her rivals' owners trudged
To fatstock show and prize inspection,
Knowing she could not be budged.

9 *Old Glamorgan*

There isn't very much to write –
I only know he's large and white .

10 *Dorset Gold Tip*

In Dorset in the days of old
There lived a pig whose hide was gold –
Friendly, beautiful, and charming,
Unsuitable for modern farming.
It can't be helped. The world moves on
And all the golden pigs are gone.

Kindness to Animals

This poem was commissioned by the editor of *The Orange Dove of Fiji*, an anthology for the benefit of the World Wide Fund for Nature. It was rejected as unsuitable.

If I went vegetarian
And didn't eat lambs for dinner,
I think I'd be a better person
And also thinner.

But the lamb is not endangered
And at least I can truthfully say
I have never, ever eaten a barn owl,
So perhaps I am OK.

Notes

ABBREVIATIONS
MC – *Making Cocoa for Kingsley Amis* (published 1986)
SC – *Serious Concerns* (published 1992)
DK – *If I Don't Know* (published 2001)

PAGE 3 'By the Round Pond'. This poem was commissioned by Dr Trevor Weston as part of a series of poems about watercolours by Peter Rodulfo. Written ?1996. *DK*.

4 'The Uncertainty of the Poet'. Commissioned by the Tate Gallery for the anthology *With a Poet's Eye* (1986) Written 1985. *SC*.

5 'The Sitter'. A Shakespearian sonnet. Commissioned by Weidenfeld and Nicolson and the Tate Gallery for the anthology *Writing on the Wall: Women Writers on Women Artists* (1993), edited by Judith Collins and Elsbeth Lindner. Written 1992. *DK*.

6 'Les Vacances'. This is a triolet (a French form that can be traced back to the thirteenth century). Commissioned by Headland Press for the anthology *The Poet's View* (1996), edited by Gladys Mary Coles. Written 1995. *DK*.
– *Maman et Papa au bord de la mer*: Mother and Papa at the seaside
– *Aujourd'hui il fait beau*: today it is fine
– *Voilà Armand*: There's Armand
– *c'est le mot*: that's the word
– *ce livre avec Mademoiselle*: this book with Mademoiselle

7 'Tich Miller'. Tich Miller was not the real name of the girl in this poem. People sometimes ask me what was wrong with her and I tell them I don't know. The teachers probably knew but they didn't tell us. Written 1982. *MC*.

8 'Names'. This is about my maternal grandmother. Written 1983. *SC*.

9 'Present'. Written 1995. *DK*.

10 'On Finding an Old Photograph'. Some readers do the arithmetic and work out that my father must have been very old when I was born, which is the case. He was one month away from his sixtieth birthday. Written *c*.1980. *MC*.

11 'A Christmas Poem'. Written 1985. *SC*.

12 'Loss'. Written 1986. *SC*.

13 'From June to December'. Excerpts from a series of ten poems. Written 1984. *MC*.

15 'My Lover'. The form is borrowed from Christopher Smart (1722–71), who used it in his lines about his cat, Jeoffrey, part of a longer poem called 'Jubilate Agno'. Smart's poem is wonderfully exuberant but I am not a cat-lover and I felt I would like to use the form to celebrate a human being. This is sometimes called a parody but I do not regard it as such. Written 1984. *MC*.

18 'Rondeau Redoublé'. I called this one by the name of its form, to make sure people understand what it is. Dorothy Parker also wrote one. She, too, called hers 'Rondeau Redoublé'. Underneath the title she added, 'And hardly worth the trouble at that.' Written 1983. *MC*.

19 'Bloody Men'. Written 1986. *SC*.

20 'Valentine'. A triolet. This acquired its title when a newspaper asked me for a poem for Valentine's Day. Written 1985. *SC*.

21 'Nine-line Triolet'. A triolet is supposed to have eight lines. This one breaks the rules a little bit because it is about breaking the rules a little bit. Written 1987. *SC*.

22 'Favourite'. Written 1987. *SC*.

23 'Another Unfortunate Choice'. A. E. Housman (1859–1936) is one of my favourite poets. He was homosexual. Although he was kind to his sisters, he seems

to have had little time for other women. A classical
scholar, he taught for a while at London University and
never learned the names of his female students. He later
moved to Cambridge, where he only had to teach men.
Written 1988. *SC*.

24 'As Sweet'. 'Narcissistic object-choice' is psychoanalytic
jargon for loving someone who reminds you of yourself.
Written 1987. *SC*.

25 'In the Rhine Valley'. This form was used by Chaucer in
the fourteenth century and is called a Chaucerian roundel.
Written 1987. *SC*.
– *Die Farben der Bäume sind schön*: The colours of the
trees are beautiful
– *Burg*: castle

26 'Postcards'. Written 1996. *DK*.
– *Grüsse aus*: greetings from
– *Mit Liebe*: with love

27 'Seeing You'. A triolet. Written 2006. Uncollected.

28 'The Orange'. Robert and Dave are former colleagues
from one of my jobs. The poem is addressed to someone
else, who is not named. Written 1989. *SC*.

29 'After the Lunch'. Written 1990. *SC*.

30 'The Aerial'. Written 1990. *SC*.

31 'Defining the Problem'. Written 1990. *SC*.

32 'Two Cures for Love'. The poet and translator Robert
Wells told me about Ovid's *Remedia Amoris* (Cures for
Love) and suggested I try and write something on the
same theme. Written 1990. *SC*.

33 'Faint Praise'. This was written as an entry for a *Spectator*
competition, which asked for verse damning a member of
the opposite sex with faint praise. When the results were
published, the judge commented that women had done
much better than men. Written 1990. *SC*.

34 'Some More Light Verse'. Written 1990. *SC*.

35 'Differences of Opinion'. I wrote both these poems in

1995. 'He Tells Her' is included in *If I Don't Know*. At the time I wrote it, I didn't want to publish 'Your Mother Knows' and I subsequently forgot all about it. Eight or nine years later I found a copy behind a bookcase. It is a pantoum. The form originated in Malaya. The two poems together, under this title, were first published in *Poetry* (USA). *DK* and uncollected.

37 'Flowers'. Written 1991. *SC*.

38 'On a Train'. Written 1999. *DK*.

39 'Being Boring'. The form I've used here is similar to a ballade. However, a ballade would have to employ the same rhymes in each stanza and have a four-line envoi at the end (see 'Proverbial Ballade', page 67). Written 1996. *DK*.

40 'Timekeeping'. Written 1997. *DK*.

41 'The Christmas Life'. Since writing this poem, I have learned that it is not a good idea to buy a Norwegian spruce. The needles drop and the tree is almost bare by Christmas. It is better to get a Nordman fir. Written 1995. *SC*.

42 '30th December'. Written 1997. *DK*.

43 'Spared'. Written a few weeks after the events of 11 September 2001. Published in the *Observer*. Uncollected.

44 'If I Don't Know'. Louise Kerr is a friend, and also our gardener. Written 1999. *DK*.

45 'Tulips'. This poem is written in Sapphic stanzas, named after the Greek poet Sappho. Written 1996. *DK*.

46 'Haiku'. Written 2006. Uncollected.

47 'Haiku: Looking Out of the Back Bedroom Window Without My Glasses'. Written 1999. *DK*.

48 'The Month of May'. A villanelle. In the course of some research for a radio programme, I learned that 'villanelle' comes from the Italian *villanella*, meaning a rustic song or dance. That discovery made me feel like writing this

poem. Written 2005. Published in *Poetry* (USA) and the
Tatler (UK). Uncollected.

49 'Leaving'. Written in the departure lounge at Los Angeles
airport, 1989. *SC*.

50 'A Nursery Rhyme: as it might have been written by
William Wordsworth'. Written 1982. *MC*.

51 'A Nursery Rhyme: as it might have been written by
T. S. Eliot'. Written 1982. *MC*.

52 'Waste Land Limericks'. One of my contributions to a
book called *How to Become Ridiculously Well-read in
One Evening*, edited by E. O. Parrott (Viking, 1985). The
idea was to rewrite any great work of English literature,
making it much shorter. Each limerick represents one of
the five sections of *The Waste Land* by T. S. Eliot. Written
1984. *MC*.

54 'A Policeman's Lot'. Can be sung to the tune of 'The
Sergeant's Song' from *The Pirates of Penzance* by Gilbert
and Sullivan ('A policeman's lot is not a happy one').
Written 1982. *MC*.

56–64 Jason Strugnell: Jason Strugnell is a poet I invented.
He began as a joke to amuse a friend, and then started to
get published. In 1980 the BBC radio producer Fraser
Steel asked me to write a dramatised feature about
Strugnell and his friends in the Tulse Hill Poetry Group.
This was broadcast on Radio 3 under the title *Shall I Call
Thee Bard?*, with Simon Jones as Strugnell. All the
Strugnell poems included here were written in the late
1970s or early in the 1980s and are in *Making Cocoa for
Kingsley Amis*.

56 'Budgie Finds His Voice'. A parody of the work of Ted
Hughes, in his 'Crow' phase. *Crow* was published in 1970.

57 'Uisce Beatha'. A parody of the work of Seamus Heaney,
written just after the publication of his collection *Field
Work* (1979). This poem was originally entitled
'Usquebaugh'. Seamus pointed out that 'usquebaugh' is

the Scottish Gaelic word for whisky, so I have changed it
to the Irish Gaelic.

58 'The Lavatory Attendant'. A parody of the work of Craig
Raine. His first book, *The Onion, Memory* (1978) opens
with a series of poems called 'Yellow Pages', describing
men with various occupations: 'The Butcher', 'The
Barber', 'The Gardener' and so on.

59 'Duffa Rex'. A parody of Geoffrey Hill's *Mercian Hymns*
(1971). In this book Hill interweaves the story of King
Offa (757–96) with material about his own childhood in
the West Midlands.

60 'God and the Jolly Bored Bog-Mouse'. This was not
entered for the Arvon competition but for a *New
Statesman* competition asking for verse that imitated the
style of all four judges. The first line of each stanza
imitates Ted Hughes, the second Philip Larkin, the third
Seamus Heaney, and the fourth Charles Causley.

61–3 'Strugnell's Sonnets'. These sonnets are dedicated to
D. M. Thomas because he suggested to me that Strugnell
should write some Shakespearean sonnets. The first line
of each is borrowed from Shakespeare, and usually
altered a bit. In the other thirteen lines Strugnell writes
about his own preoccupations in his own way. The
sonnets are not parodies of Shakespeare.

– Sonnet I: 'Th'expense of spirit in a waste of shame'
(Shakespeare, Sonnet 129). The selection of wine
available in Tesco has improved considerably since I
wrote this poem.

– Sonnet IV: 'Not marble, nor the gilded monuments'
(Shakespeare, Sonnet 55). O-levels were the exams my
generation took instead of GCSEs.

– Sonnet VII: 'Alas 'tis true, I have gone here and there'
(Shakespeare, Sonnet 110). I sent this to Andrew Motion
before it was published. He was very good-natured about
it.

64 'Strugnell's Haiku'. There is more to writing haiku than counting syllables and making sure there are seventeen of them. Strugnell's attempts to imitate the Japanese masters remind me of some of the failed efforts I have seen in schools and elsewhere.

65 'Reading Berryman's *Dream Songs* at the Writers' Retreat'. John Berryman was born in Oklahoma in 1914 and committed suicide in 1972 after a long struggle with depression and alcoholism. His book *The Dream Songs* comprises 385 poems, each of them eighteen lines long. The poems are about a character called Henry, assumed to be Berryman, detailing the ups and downs of his everyday life. Henry has a sidekick, never named, who addresses him as Mr Bones – a device borrowed from minstrel shows. Hawthornden Castle is a writers' retreat outside Edinburgh. I spent a month there in 1993 and wrote several poems, including this one. *DK*.

66 'Reading Scheme'. A poem that arose from my work as a primary-school teacher. It makes fun of the *Ladybird* reading scheme, as it was in the 1970s, and of other reading schemes of the time. It is a villanelle. I chose this repetitive form because reading schemes are repetitive. Written *c*.1980. *MC*.

67 'Proverbial Ballade'. As the title says, this is a ballade (not to be confused with a ballad). The ballade first appeared in Provençal literature and was, most famously, used by François Villon in the fifteenth century. By that time the form had already found its way into English literature in the work of Chaucer and Gower. This poem was inspired by a *New Statesman* competition asking for wise-sounding but meaningless proverbs. The competition was so successful that the magazine ran it more than once. I wrote dozens of silly proverbs, far too many to send in to the *New Statesman*, so I decided to put some of them into a poem. Written 1980. *MC*.

69 'Exchange of Letters'. Written 1983. *SC*.

71 'Stress'. The meaning of some English words only becomes clear when we hear where the stress falls. For example, 'col*lect*', with the stress on the second syllable, is a verb; '*coll*ect', with the stress on the first syllable, is a noun meaning a kind of prayer. My friend Henry Thompson made a list of such words and I decided to put some of them into a sonnet. I wanted to dedicate the poem to him without seeming to suggest that the unpleasant man in the poem is anything like Henry. I borrowed an idea from John Betjeman, whose poem 'The Wykehamist' includes the line 'a rather dirty Wykehamist'; the dedication reads 'To Randolph Churchill, but not about him.' Written 2000. *DK*.

72 'An Attempt at Unrhymed Verse'. This isn't in any of my collections because it was considered to be a poem for children. It has appeared in several children's anthologies. However, I include it in all my readings to adult audiences and I can't see any good reason not to include it here. Written early 1980s. Uncollected.

73 'Making Cocoa for Kingsley Amis'. Sir Kingsley Amis (1922–95) was the author of more than twenty novels, including the ever popular *Lucky Jim* (1954) and *The Old Devils*, which won the Booker Prize in 1986. He also published several books of poems. More than once in the 1980s he said in newspaper articles that he wished there were more new young poets who could use rhyme and metre. I hoped someone would tell him about me. One evening I found myself at a reception where Amis was also a guest. I wanted to meet him but didn't dare go up and speak to him. That night I dreamed I was making him a cup of cocoa. When I woke up I found the dream amusing because it was fairly well known that cocoa was not the author's favourite drink (he preferred whisky). Then I wrote the poem. Written *c*.1984. *MC*.

74 'Sonnet of '68'. In 1969 Harry Oberländer became a
student in Frankfurt and got involved in the wave of
student protest, sometimes called the movement of '68.
'Those who did not outgrow it' is a reference to activists
who were killed, like the student Benno Ohnesorg, shot in
1967 by a policeman in Berlin during the state visit of the
Shah of Iran, or like one of the leaders of the protests,
Rudi Dutschke, who was the victim of an assassination
attempt and died of his injuries in 1979. These events
pushed some in the student movement towards
increasingly extremist violence and the formation of the
Red Army Faction (also known as the Baader-Meinhof
gang), which was responsible for several bombings and
murders. Several of the leading members of this group
committed suicide in prison in the 1970s. Others were
killed before they could be arrested. Oberländer wrote
this sonnet in the 1980s. The original German version,
Das Achtundsechziger-Sonett, was included in his book
Garten Eden, Achterbahn (Giessen, Edition Literarischer
Salon, 1988). Translated 1987. *DK*.

75 'Anniversary Poem'. This was commissioned by a canon
of St Paul's cathedral (a woman) to be read at a service to
celebrate the tenth anniversary of the ordination of the
first women priests in the Church of England. It wasn't
used because, although the women at St Paul's enjoyed it,
it was felt that the humour was 'too robust'. I saw their
point. My anger about the way women priests have
sometimes been treated inevitably got into the poem,
making it unsuitable for a celebration. I couldn't have
written a less angry poem on the subject, and I don't
regret writing this one. The first lines of stanzas 2, 3, 4
and 5 use language borrowed from the Psalms. Written
2003. Published in *Poetry* (USA). Uncollected.

76 'How to Deal with the Press'. A villanelle. Written ?1996.
DK.

77 'A Hampshire Disaster'. Nobody was hurt in the fire at the Royal Winchester Golf Club in 1994. If they had been, I would not have allowed myself to make fun of the language I found in the *Hampshire Chronicle* report. Written 1994. *DK*.

78 'Greek Island Triolets'. Written at the Skyros Centre in 1994. *DK*.

79 'Limerick'. When Brooke Bond stopped using chimpanzees in its advertisements for PG Tips, I realised this poem's days were numbered. Written 1980. Uncollected.

80 'The Stickleback Song'. This arose from an inspection of the London primary school I was working in at the time. An inspector really did make the mysterious comment quoted at the top. It was before the days of Ofsted: inspections were less arduous and intimidating than they subsequently became. Even so, a General Inspection was something of an ordeal and I thought my colleagues might be glad of some light relief. Written 1984. *DK*.

82 'Traditional Prize County Pigs'. This was inspired by a calendar of pigs. There were, of course, twelve pigs on the calendar but I could only manage to write poems about ten of them. Written 1997. *DK*.

86 'Kindness to Animals'. Written 1988. *SC*.